Platinum

12 COOL SONGS from
Jerald's COOL SONGS Series
(visit musicmotivation.com/coolsongs to learn more)

For Intermediate - Late Intermediate Piano Students

Music Mentor

JERALD SIMON

Music Motivation®™

Cool music that excites, entertains, and educates!™

visit http://musicmotivation.com
follow Jerald on Facebook: https://facebook.com/jeraldsimon
subscribe to Jerald's YouTube page: https://youtube.com/jeraldsimon

Music Motivation® books are designed to provide students with music instruction that will enable them to improve and increase their successes in the field of music. It is also intended to enhance appreciation and understanding of various styles of music from classical to jazz, blues, rock, popular, new age, hymns, and more. The author and publisher disclaim any liability or accountability for the misuse of this material as it was intended by the author.

I hope you enjoy "Platinum." With this book, I hope that piano teachers and piano students have fun! Each "Cool Song" teaches the theory, concept, or skill for which they were created. More important, I want the students to have a good time playing these. These are great as student savers and very fun performance pieces any student would want to play and perform. Minus tracks can be used as well. You will hear the accompaniment music at three speeds: (1) Performance Speed with Piano, (2) Performance Speed - No Piano, and (3) Practice Speed - No Piano.

Your Music Mentor™ Jerald Simon

Introduction...3
Super Sonic Boom...8
New Wave..10
New Heights...12
Hybrid Hero 14
Synthesis...16
Sonic..18
Sonic Fusion 20
Power Play...22
Eclectic...24
Hard Core...26
Platinum...28
Road Trip..30
More best sellers by Jerald
Learn more about Jerald

This book is dedicated to the many YouTube subscribers who watch my videos on my YouTube page (youtube.com/jeraldsimon) Also, for my wife, Suzanne (Zanny), my sweet daughter, Summer, and my two sons, Preston, and Matthew.

The front and background image is from the website: http://www.istockphoto.com - Copyright ©iStock.com/jaskoomerovic

CONNECT with Jerald

http://musicmotivation.com/jeraldsimon
https://facebook.com/jeraldsimon
http://youtube.com/jeraldsimon
http://linkedin.com/in/jeraldsimon
http://pinterest.com/jeraldsimon
https://twitter.com/jeraldsimon
http://cdbaby.com/artist/jeraldsimon
http://instagram.com/jeraldsimon
jeraldsimon@musicmotivation.com

CONTACT Music Motivation®

Music Motivation®™

Cool music that excites, entertains, and educates!™

Music Motivation®
P.O. Box 1000
Kaysville, UT 84037-1000
http://musicmotivation.com
https://facebook.com/musicmotivation
https://twitter.com/musicmotivation
info@musicmotivation.com

First Printing 2015 - Printed in the United States of America - 10 9 8 7 6 5 4 3 2 1 - Simon, Jerald - Music Motivation® - Platinum - $18.95 US/ $20.95 Canada - Soft cover spiral bound book - ISBN-13: MM00001020

Music Motivation® is a registered ® trademark

Welcome to "Platinum" by JERALD SIMON

All 12 of these cool songs were composed by Jerald Simon as part of his "Cool Songs Series." Here is a description of Jerald's COOL SONGS Series:

"Jerald Simon composes 'Cool Songs' to teach students the theory of the new piece with fun examples/exercises that demonstrate the practical application of learning music theory, so students can begin making music of their own."

If you would like to learn more about Jerald's weekly "Cool Songs" from his annual subscription, you can visit his website at **musicmotivation.com/coolsongs** for more information.

"My purpose and mission in life is to motivate myself and others through my music and writing, to help others find their purpose and mission in life, and to teach values that encourage everyone everywhere to do and be their best." - Jerald Simon

A message from Jerald to piano students and parents:

If you come to piano lessons each week and walk away only having learned about music notation, rhythm, and dots on a page, then I have failed as a Music Mentor. Life lessons are just as important, if not more important than music lessons. I would rather have you learn more about goal setting and achieving, character, dedication, and personal improvement. To have you learn to love music, appreciate it, and play it, is a wonderful byproduct you will have for the rest of your life - a talent that will enrich your life and the lives of others. To become a better musician is wonderful and important, but to become a better person is more important.

As a Music Mentor I want to mentor students to be the very best they can be. If you choose not to practice, you essentially choose not to improve. This is true in any area of life. Everyone has the same amount of time allotted to them. What you choose to do with your time, and where you spend your time, has little to do with the activities being done and more to do with the value attached to each activity.

I believe it's important to be well-rounded and have many diverse interests. I want students to enjoy music, to learn to be creative and understand how to express themselves musically - either by creating music of their own, or interpreting the music of others - by arranging and improvising well known music. In addition, I encourage students to play sports, dance, sing, draw, read, and develop all of their talents. I want them to be more than musicians, I want them to learn to become well-rounded individuals.

Above all, I want everyone to continually improve and do their best. I encourage everyone to set goals, dream big, and be the best they can be in whatever they choose to do. Life is full of wonderful choices. Choose the best out of life and learn as much as you can from everyone everywhere. I prefer being called a Music Mentor because I want to mentor others and help them to live their dreams.

Your life is your musical symphony. Make it a masterpiece!

JERALD SIMON

Many piano teachers, piano students, and parents of piano students ask me how or why I began creating the "Cool Songs" from my **"Cool Songs Subscription"** (musicmotivation.com/coolsongs). It began with my "Cool Songs for Cool Kids" Series (Primer Level and Books 1, 2, and 3), and my "Cool Songs that ROCK!" Series (books 1 and 2). To be honest, however, it actually began long before any of those books were created.

I began teaching piano lessons part time in 2003, I was newly married and was selling pianos in a piano store. I didn't start teaching full time as an independant piano teacher until 2006. Between 2003 and 2006 I had a few different sales jobs I did as well, while continuing to do things on the side for my music career. In 2006 I created my music company, **Music Motivation**®, at first for my piano studio and for me as a performing musician. I then felt motivated to come out with two books back to back. The first book I ever created was "An Introduction to Scales and Modes". It is an in-depth tutorial of basic scales and modes in all key signatures. After that I came out with my second book, "Variations on Mary Had a Little Lamb." This book has nine different arrangements I created using the children's song, "Mary Had a Little Lamb." These are some of the arrangements in the book: Mary Took Her Lamb to a Swingin' Jazz Club, Mary's Lamb Had the Blues, Mary Took Her Lamb to a 50s Rock Concert, Mary and Her Lamb Live with Indians, etc., etc., until the last arrangement of: Mary Took Her Lamb to a Funeral.

These books were created to help students learn the theory and the practical application of the music. As a result of these two books, my piano studio more than doubled. At my most busy time in teaching, I had around 88 piano students. The majority were teenage boys (ages 11-19), and most of them wanted to quit piano lessons. Piano teachers and parents of piano students would send me their students who essentially wanted nothing more to do with the instrument. The parents and teachers said they didn't want their students to quit and asked me to try to motivate them to keep playing the piano (I guess that is what I get for naming my company Music Motivation®). The students would not play from any method book past or present and would never suggest music they wanted to play. I needed to figure out how to reach these students and connect with them. I asked each of them what kind of music they enjoyed and asked them to bring it so they could work on it. The majority would not do it. I then asked them to challenge me to create or compose a piano solo for them during their lesson. They all found this very entertaining. I would tell them to choose a style of music, key signature, and the time signature. With some pieces, such as "Game Over" from "Cool Songs for Cool Kids" book 1, they even said I could only use four notes. It was a game for the students and a challenge for me. With each of these students, I composed a piano solo during their lesson time and even notated it in Finale. At the end of their lesson I printed off the music and sent it home with them. I challenged them to learn the piano solo and then let me know what they thought. I told them I would compose a new piece the following week during their next lesson for them.

It worked! The following week, the students returned and I asked them if they had tried to play it. The majority of these students had not only tried to play it, but had perfected the piece and said they were ready to challenge me to compose a new piano solo. I would accept their challenge and tell them they would need to play what I composed. I asked the students what they honestly thought about the music and almost without exception, the students said they thought the music sounded "cool." They told me they would play the piano more if they could have more "cool" sounding music like the piano solo I had composed. I appreciated their positive feedback. I told them I would emphasize the music theory in the "cool song" because they need to know their music theory, but I also told them I wanted them to have fun learning these "cool songs" each week. That is how it all began. All of the "cool songs" I had composed in each lesson were later compiled into "Cool Songs for Cool Kids" books 1, 2, and 3. Because of the great feedback of these books, I then created "Cool Songs that ROCK!" books 1 and 2 for older teenagers that were a little more advanced. I have my students play through all of the "cool songs" I create so I can receive their feedback . They know what they like and what sounds "cool" to them. I listen to and now receive feedback from many piano teachers, piano students, and parents of piano students around the world who tell me what they would like me to compose as well. Have fun with this music!

The *Music Motivation*® Mentorship Map (for piano students)
by Music Mentor™ Jerald Simon

Music Motivation®
musicmotivation.com

MOTIVATION

	♪ Apprentice ♪ for 1st & 2nd year students	♪ Maestro ♪ for 2nd - 4th year students	♪ Virtuoso ♪ for 3rd year students and above
Repertoire *In addition to the books listed to the right, students can sign up to receive the weekly "Cool Song" and "Cool Exercise" composed by Jerald Simon every week. Visit musicmotivation.com annual subscription to learn more and sign up!*	**Music Motivation® Book(s)** What Every Pianist Should Know (Free PDF) Essential Piano Exercises (section 1) The Pentascale Pop Star Cool Songs for Cool Kids (primer level) Cool Songs for Cool Kids (book 1) Songs in Pentascale position: Classical, Jazz, Blues, Popular, Students Choice, Personal Composition (in pentascale position - 5 note piano solo) etc.	**Music Motivation® Book(s)** Essential Piano Exercises (section 2), & New Age An Introduction to Scales and Modes Cool Songs for Cool Kids (book 2) Cool Songs for Cool Kids (book 3) Variations on Mary Had a Little Lamb Twinkle Those Stars, Jazzed about Christmas, Jazzed about 4th of July Baroque, Romantic, Classical, Jazz, Blues, Popular, New Age, Student's Choice, Personal Composition.	**Music Motivation® Book(s)** Essential Piano Exercises (section 3), & Jazz EPE Cool Songs that ROCK! (books 1 & 2) Triumphant, Sea Fever, Sweet Melancholy, The Dawn of a New Age, Sweet Modality, Jazzed about Jazz, Jazzed about Classical Music, Jingle Those Bells, Cinematic Solos, Hymn Arranging Baroque, Romantic, Classical, Jazz, Blues, Popular, New Age, Contemporary, Broadway Show Tunes, Standards, Student's Choice, Personal Composition
Music Terminology	Piano (*p*), Forte (*f*) Mezzo Piano (*mp*) Mezzo Forte (*mf*) Pianissimo (*pp*) Fortissimo (*ff*) ***Music Motivation® 1st Year Terminology***	Tempo Markings Dynamic Markings Parts of the Piano Styles and Genres of Music ***Music Motivation® 2nd Year Terminology***	Pocket Music Dictionary (2 - 3 years) Harvard Dictionary of Music (4 + years) Parts/History of the Piano Music Composers (Weekly Biographies) ***Music Motivation® 3rd Year Terminology***
Key Signatures	C, G, D, A, F, B♭, E♭ & A♭ (Major) A, E, B, F♯, D, G, C & F (Minor) Begin learning all major key signatures	Circle of 5ths/Circle of 4ths <u>All</u> Major and Minor key signatures (Identify each key and name the sharps and flats)	Spiral of Fifths, Chord Progressions within Key Signatures. Modulating from one Key Signature to another.
Music Notation	Names and Positions of notes on the staff (both hands - Treble and Bass Clefs)	Names and Positions of notes above and below the staff (both hands)	History of Music Notation (the development of notation), Monks & Music, Gregorian Chants, Music changes over the years and how music has changed. Learn **Finale** and **Logic Pro** (notate your music)
Rhythms	<u>Whole notes/rests</u> (say it and play it - count out loud) <u>Half notes/rests</u> (say it and play it - count out loud) <u>Quarter notes/rests</u> (say it and play it - count out loud) <u>Eighth notes/rests</u> (say it and play it - count out loud)	<u>Sixteenth notes/rests</u> (say it and play it - count out loud) <u>Thirty-second notes/rests</u> (say it and play it - count out loud) <u>Sixty-fourth notes/rests</u> (say it and play it - count out loud)	<u>One-hundred-twenty-eighth notes/rests</u> For more on rhythm, I recommend: "Rhythmic Training" by Robert Starer and "Logical Approach to Rhythmic Notation" (books 1 & 2) by Phil Perkins
Intervals	1st, 2nd, 3rd, 4th, 5th, 6th, 7th, 8th, and 9th intervals (key of C, G, D, F, B♭, and E♭). Harmonic and Melodic intervals (key of C, G, D, A, E, and B)	<u>All</u> Perfect, Major, Minor, Augmented, and Diminished intervals (in every key) <u>All</u> Harmonic and Melodic intervals Explain the intervals used to create major, minor, diminished, and augmented chords?	9th, 11th, and 13th intervals Analyze music (Hymns and Classical) to identify intervals used in each measure. Identify/Name intervals used in chords.
Scales	<u>All</u> Major Pentascales (5 finger scale) <u>All</u> Minor Pentascales (5 finger scale) <u>All</u> Diminished Pentascales (5 finger scale) C Major Scale (1 octave) A min. Scale (1 oct.) (Do, Re, Mi, Fa, Sol, La, Ti, Do) (solfege) All Major and Natural Minor Scales - 1 octave	<u>All</u> Major Scales (Every Key 1 - 2 octaves) <u>All</u> Minor Scales (Every Key 1 - 2 octaves) (natural, harmonic, and melodic minor scales) (Do, Di, Re, Ri, Mi, Fa, Fi, Sol, Si, La, Li, Ti, Do) (solfege - chromatic)	<u>All</u> Major Scales (Every Key 3 - 5 Octaves) <u>All</u> Minor Scales (Every Key 3 - 5 Octaves) <u>All</u> Blues Scales (major and minor) Cultural Scales (25 + scales)
Modes	Ionian/Aeolian (C/A, G/E, D/B, A/F♯)	<u>All</u> Modes (I, D, P, L, M, A, L) <u>All</u> keys	Modulating with the Modes (Dorian to Dorian)
Chords	<u>All</u> Major Chords, <u>All</u> Minor Chords, <u>All</u> Diminished Chords, C Sus 2, C Sus 4, C+ (Aug)., C 6th, C minor 6th, C 7th, C Maj. 7th, C minor Major 7th, A min., A Sus 2, A Sus 4,	<u>All</u> Major, Minor, Diminished, Augmented, Sus 2, Sus 4, Sixth, Minor Sixth, Dominant 7th and Major 7th Chords	Review <u>All</u> Chords from 1st and 2nd year experiences <u>All</u> 7th, 9th, 11th, and 13th chords inversions and voicings.
Arpeggios	Same chords as above (1 - 2 octaves)	Same chords as above (3 - 4 octaves)	Same chords as above (4 + octaves)
Inversions	Same chords as above (1 - 2 octaves)	Same chords as above (3 - 4 octaves)	Same chords as above (4 + octaves)
Technique (other)	Schmitt Preparatory Exercises, (Hanon)	Wieck, Hanon, Bach (well tempered clavier)	Bertini-Germer, Czerny, I. Philipp
Sight Reading	Key of C Major and G Major	Key of C, G, D, A, E, F, B♭, E♭, A♭, D♭	<u>All</u> Key Signatures, Hymns, Classical
Ear Training	Major versus Minor sounds (chords/intervals)	C, D, E, F, G, A, B, and intervals	Key Signatures and Chords, Play w/ IPod
Music History	The origins of the Piano Forte	Baroque, Classical, Jazz, Blues	Students choice - <u>All</u> genres, Composers
Improvisation	Mary Had a Little Lamb, Twinkle, Twinkle...	Blues Pentascale, Barrelhouse Blues	Classical, New Age, Jazz, Blues, etc. Play w/ IPod
Composition	5 note melody (both hands - key of C and G)	One - Two Page Song (include key change)	Lyrical, Classical, New Age, Jazz, etc.

A few theory FUNdamentals to work on! (practice these)

Whenever I have students work on a new piece, I always ask them to first tell me the key signature and how many sharps or flats there are (and which ones), the time signature, dynamics, and what they think of the piece just from looking at it. To find the key signature, look at the first measure of the piece and see how many sharps or flats there are. With sharps, you will find the last sharp (the one farthest to the right), and will go up half a step to find out which key it is in. Look below at the third example on this page. There are two sharps. Look at the last one that is farthest to the right, C sharp, and go up half a step above that. This is the key of D Major (two sharps - F sharp and C sharp). To find the key signature when dealing with flats, simply find the second to last flat, and that is your key signature. The time signature is in the first measure of the piece and has two numbers stacked one on top the other (e.g. 2/4, 4/4, 6/8, etc.).

This is the left hand pattern from Super Sonic Boom (measure 1) on page 8. We are in the key of E flat major (three flats - B flat, E flat, and A flat), and the left hand plays a pattern created from the chromatic scale (which is the half step scale). Try this example! It's an interesting sound I think you'll enjoy!

Try playing the first two measures from New Wave on page 10. This piece is in the key of C Major. The right hand plays three note chords while the left hand plays an octave interval. Can you create a "Cool Song" of your own by using the chord progression in these two measures? Play around with it and see what you can do.

The example above shows measures 11-15 from the piano piece "New Heights" on page 12. It is in a 4/4 time signature. Again, the left hand is playing an octave interval (octave means eight: i.e. C-C), while the right hand plays several octave chords (some are suspended). "New Heights" is in the key of D Major.

A few theory FUNdamentals to work on! (practice these)

The example below shows measures 10-14 from the piano piece "Synthesis" on page 16. It is in a 4/4 time signature. This piece is in the key of C Major and primarily uses a fifth interval with the left hand and the basic triad with the right hand. Play the example below and then look at the next exercise/example.

Now play all of the triads created from the C Major scale (all in root position) moving up the scale. You have C Major, D minor, E minor, F Major, G Major, A minor, B diminished, and C Major. The left hand is playing the accompanying perfect 5th interval that relates to the triad played with the right hand.

Pretty easy, huh? Now that you can play that, try to *play the exact same six measures from above in all key signatures.* You can follow the **Circle of 5ths, the circle/cycle of 4ths,** or simply move up chromatically in half steps. Since we are using the triads created from the major scale, let's start off by following the **Circle of 5ths.** This then becomes your order for the key signatures you will play (these are not chords, but are the corresponding key signatures and order in which to use them):

C Major - G Major - D Major - A Major - E Major - B Major - F sharp Major - C sharp Major

Going backwards you can follow the **Circle/Cycle of 4ths** as follows:

C Major - F Major - B flat Major - E flat Major - A flat Major - D flat Major - G flat Major - C flat Major

The whole point of this exercise is to have you try to transpose a few measures and play the same thing in all key signatures without looking at the music. You can do this. If you take the exercise above and play it in the key of G Major, as an example, the order of your triads played with the right hand would be:

G Major, A minor, B minor, C Major, D Major, E minor, F sharp diminished, G Major

Try to play this in all keys. Have fun with this!

SUPER SONIC BOOM

This fun "cool song" is in the key of C minor - the relative minor to E flat major. See if you can create your own cool song using the left hand pattern in this piece. Can you use intervals with the right hand (e.g. 1st = C, 2nd = C and D, 3rd = C and E flat, 4th = C and F, 5th = C and G, 6th = C and A flat, 7th = C and B flat, and 8th = C and C)? Try playing triads or three note chords with the right hand. Have fun playing this!

Watch the YouTube video of Jerald playing this by visiting his YouTube page: youtube.com/jeraldsimon. It is one of the "Cool Songs" videos under the "Platinum by Jerald Simon" playlist. You may also type in "Super Sonic Boom by Jerald Simon" in the YouTube search box to find the video as well.

BY JERALD SIMON

Better Watch out for the Sonic Boom! (M.M. ♩ = c. 120)

9

New Wave

This fun "cool song" was created to help students learn a few things. First, the left hand is only playing octave intervals. Students should try playing all octave intervals moving up and down the piano in half steps (chromatically). Secondly, the right hand is playing triads or three note chords, but most of them are not in root position. In measure one the right hand plays the C major chord in second inversion and then plays the F major chord in first inversion. In measure two we can refer to the first chord as an A minor seventh chord or as the C major/A slash chord. Have fun playing this!

Watch the YouTube video of Jerald playing this by visiting his YouTube page: youtube.com/jeraldsimon. It is one of the "Cool Songs" videos under the "Platinum by Jerald Simon" playlist. You may also type in "New Wave by Jerald Simon" in the YouTube search box to find the video as well.

BY JERALD SIMON

New Wave

NEW HEIGHTS

This fun "cool song" was created to give the students a fun scaler piece. The first seven measures of the piece feature the right hand playing a D major scale up and down one octave. Starting in measure eight, the left hand plays quarter note octave intervals while the right hand plays octave chords. Have FUN practicing/playing the D major scale and the octave intervals and octave chords created from the D major scale!

Watch the YouTube video of Jerald playing this by visiting his YouTube page: youtube.com/jeraldsimon. It is one of the "Cool Songs" videos under the "Platinum by Jerald Simon" playlist. You may also type in "New Heights by Jerald Simon" in the YouTube search box to find the video as well.

BY JERALD SIMON

NEW HEIGHTS

Hybrid Hero

This fun "cool song" was created to help students learn to keep rhythmn with competing eighth notes and eighth rests between the right and left hand. Have FUN playing this chord progression!

Watch the YouTube video of Jerald playing this by visiting his YouTube page: youtube.com/jeraldsimon. It is one of the "Cool Songs" videos under the "Platinum by Jerald Simon" playlist. You may also type in "Hybrid Hero by Jerald Simon" in the YouTube search box to find the video as well.

BY JERALD SIMON

Hybrid Hero

Can you name the intervals from measures 24-32 with the right hand?

15

SYNTHESIS

This fun "cool song" was created to help students learn a simple chord progression of C major to A minor, F major, and G major. This is commonly known by roman numerals as I-vi-IV-V (1-6-4-5) Half way through the piece we change the order of the chord progression to be vi-IV-I-V (6-4-1-5) so the students can practice playing around with the chords. Have fun playing this chord progression!

Watch the YouTube video of Jerald playing this by visiting his YouTube page: youtube.com/jeraldsimon. It is one of the "Cool Songs" videos under the "Platinum by Jerald Simon" playlist. You may also type in "Synthesis by Jerald Simon" in the YouTube search box to find the video as well.

Students can write in their own dynamics with this piece!

BY JERALD SIMON

SYNTHESIS

To learn more about Jerald's cool weekly songs and cool exercises,
please visit musicmotivation.com/coolsongs

SONIC

This fun "cool song" was created to have students learn a minor chord progression of A minor, F major, and G major. The students practice playing the individual notes, then the octave intervals, followed by the notes as eighth notes and then as broken fifth intervals followed by blocked fifth and fourth intervals beginning in measure 17. Starting in measure 21, students play the chords in various inversions. Have fun playing intervals!!

Watch the YouTube video of Jerald playing this by visiting his YouTube page: youtube.com/jeraldsimon. It is one of the "Cool Songs" videos under the "Platinum by Jerald Simon" playlist. You may also type in "Sonic by Jerald Simon" in the YouTube search box to find the video as well.

BY JERALD SIMON

SONIC

SONIC FUSION

This fun "cool song" was created to teach a steady "ROCK" style and left hand pattern. The left hand plays an octave chord where the third interval has been left out (e.g. A E A is an A minor octave chord where the C note, or third interval, has been left out). Have FUN playing this ROCK piano piece!

Watch the YouTube video of Jerald playing this by visiting his YouTube page: youtube.com/jeraldsimon. It is one of the "Cool Songs" videos under the "Platinum by Jerald Simon" playlist. You may also type in "Sonic Fusion by Jerald Simon" in the YouTube search box to find the video as well.

BY JERALD SIMON

SONIC FUSION

21

Power Play

This fun "cool song" was created to teach three simple chords to piano students: C Suspend the 2nd, (C Sus2), C Major (C), and C Csuspend the 4th (C Sus4 or sometimes simply C Sus)

Watch the YouTube video of Jerald playing this by visiting his YouTube page: youtube.com/jeraldsimon. It is one of the "Cool Songs" videos under the "Platinum by Jerald Simon" playlist. You may also type in "Power Play by Jerald Simon" in the YouTube search box to find the video as well.

BY JERALD SIMON

17 C sus/F C/F C sus2/F C/F C sus C C sus2 C
21 C sus/G C/G C sus2/F C/F C sus C C sus2 C
mf
25 C sus2/G C/G C sus/G C/G C sus/F C/F C sus2/F C/F
29 C sus2 C C sus/F C/F C sus2 C C sus/F C/F
mp
33 C sus2/G C/G C sus/F C sus2/F C
f

Eclectic

This fun "cool song" is in the key of E flat major. The left hand is primarily using a perfect 5th interval. The right hand is using several third intervals and triads (three note chords). I intentionally left out the dynamic markings because I want students to write their own dynamic markings in to the piece and play this the way they would like to. Have fun playing this!

Watch the YouTube video of Jerald playing this by visiting his YouTube page: youtube.com/jeraldsimon. It is one of the "Cool Songs" videos under the "Platinum by Jerald Simon" playlist. You may also type in "Eclectic by Jerald Simon" in the YouTube search box to find the video as well.

Like a Pop Star (M.M. ♩ = c. 120)

BY JERALD SIMON

Students can write in their own dynamics!

pedal ad-lib

Eclectic

Hard Core

This fun "cool song" is in the key of E minor (the relative minor to G major). We have quite a few interesting rhythms in this piece. It begins with triplets against half notes and then in measure 5 we also introduce something that looks a little scary, but it isn't too difficult. It is 5 against 1. This is the quintuplet. In this case, 5 sixteenth notes equal one quarter note.

Watch the YouTube video of Jerald playing this by visiting his YouTube page: youtube.com/jeraldsimon. It is one of the "Cool Songs" videos under the "Platinum by Jerald Simon" playlist.

With Power and Intensity (M.M. ♩ = c. 120)

BY JERALD SIMON

pedal ad-lib throughout

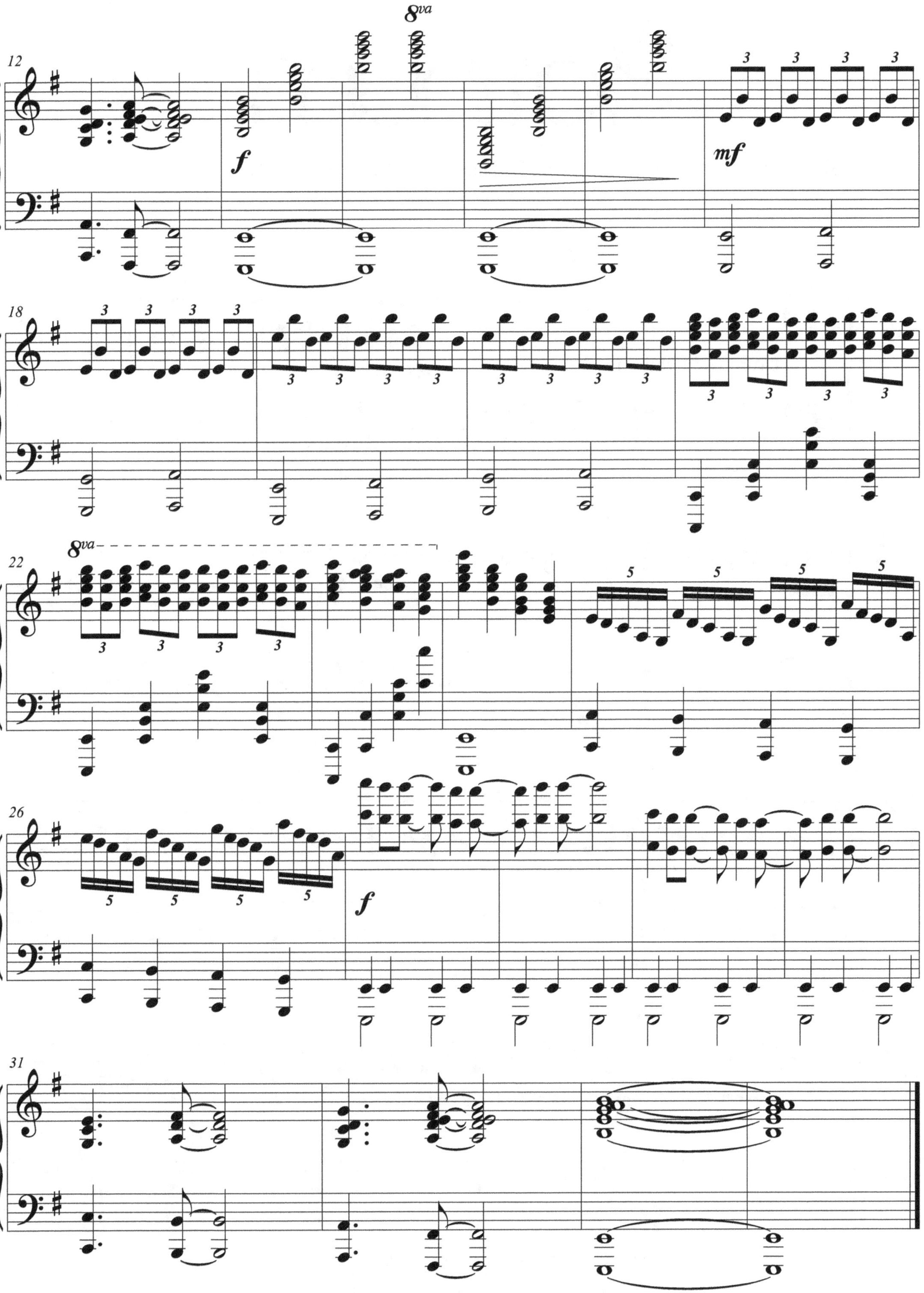
12
8va
f
mf
18
22
8va
26
f
31

Platinum

Skill - Pop Chord Progression: Am - F major - C major - G major - Have fun playing this!

By Jerald Simon

Platinum

29

Road Trip

Skill - Left hand (octave) rock pattern. Try this on any note on the Piano! (see measure 17)

A Rock Feel (M.M. ♩ = c. 120)

BY JERALD SIMON

Road Trip

I'd love to have you learn more of my piano music I have composed. Most have been dubbed 'COOL SONGS!' So WHAT are COOL SONGS? And WHY do thousands of piano teachers worldwide use them and rave about them so much? What's the BIG deal? To learn more about my cool songs and cool exercises, please visit **musicmotivation.com/coolsongs** and **essentialpianoexercises.com**

Currently there are over 163 COOL SONGS in the COOL SONGS series - complete with video lessons and accompaniment minus tracks in three separate levels:

The Apprentice Stage (beginning level)
The Maestro Stage (early intermediate level)
The Virtuoso Stage (late intermediate - advanced levels)

My Mission: (*My Primary Music Motivation® Goal*): Create fun, original piano music that is cool, exciting, entertaining, and educational to help motivate and inspire piano students! (especially teenage boys)!

My Music Motivation® Goal (for music educators): One of my primary goals at Music Motivation® is to help prepare the next generation of composers, arrangers, musicians, music teachers, and musicologists to use their music and their love of music to make a difference in their own lives, their community, and the world.

Music Motivation® is dedicated to motivating music students of all ages with "Music that excites, entertains, and educates". The three main areas of focus for Music Motivation® are: Theory Therapy, Innovative Improvisation, and Creative Composition.

Want more FUN and COOL sounding piano music?
Download this **FREE PDF book** -
"20 Ways to Motivate Teen Piano Students to Want to Play the Piano" at:
https://www.musicmotivation.com/optin.

To learn more about Jerald's cool songs and cool exercises,
please visit **musicmotivation.com/coolsongs**

As a music student, decide what you would like to do with your music. How can you share your talent with others? What style of music would you like to learn in addition to what you are learning?

As a music teacher, decide how you can inspire and motivate your music students to set and achieve their own personal goals. Lead by example. Determine what more you would like to do with your music and start doing what you have always dreamed of doing.

As a parent, help your children understand the importance of setting and achieving goals. Write down the personal goals you'd like to achieve in your own life. Sit down with your children and discuss the importance of goals in their lives. Come up with personal goals and a game plan of how you will achieve them. Write down 1, 2, 5, 10, 15, and 20 year plans. Be very specific. Make goals a daily habit for you and your children.

If you would like to learn more about goal setting, I have created a course titled, **"Empowered by Positivity!"** There are two separate courses, one for teens and one for adults. You can learn more about this course at the following links:

Empowered by Positivity for TEENS: https://www.empoweredbypositivity.com/empowered-by-positivity-course-for-teens

Empowered by Positivity for ADULTS: https://www.empoweredbypositivity.com/empowered-by-positivity-course

When you visit either of these links, you'll be able to download a FREE PDF book I wrote, **"Who Are You? Your Personal Success Goal Book."** The online course is about becoming who you were born to be!

It also features and includes my books, **"Perceptions, Parables, and Pointers," "The 'As If' Principle" (motivational poetry), and "Poetry that Motivates."**

In this course, you will learn about my "Stepping Stones for Success" - Becoming Who You Were Born to Be. You will also have access to my "How to Experience More Peace and Positivity in Life" - How to Transform Your Life by Embracing the Sweetness of Simplicity - the 60 Day Challenge to Change Your Perspective and Experience Inner Peace.

Set goals for yourself every day. Learn as much as you can about self improvement and how to be better today than you were yesterday. You have so many wonderful opportunities to learn and grow and stretch yourself to do amazing things in life

Take time each day to review what you have accomplished and what more you hope to accomplish as well. You can and will do so much in your life. Never live with regrets for what you failed to accomplish or never attempted to do in the first place. The best experiences in life come about because you lived life to the fullest and pushed yourself to do more and be more.

Goals will help give you direction and you will know more perfectly how to become the person you were born to be. It is a life journey and you are beginning the journey of a lifetime. It is your own personal progression from where you are to the destinations you have dreamed of visiting. Do your very best!

Let's talk a little more intentionally about goal setting with your music. Most people have never thought about goal setting as a day to day part of life. In my opinion, you set goals and it becomes a habit. We can predict where we want to go and how we will arrive at our pre-determined destination. What is the big picture? Where do we see ourselves in our short-term and long-term future? We can decide what we would like to do with our lives and where we want to go, but first, we must dream and plan for the future.

There are many goal areas that need our focus and attention.

If you have never thought about setting goals, either because you are young or because it has never seemed important, please begin today. The great thing about music is that it actually falls into all seven of these areas. Each of these goal areas is affected by music, and music has an effect on each of them. As a musician, you can be as effective or ineffective as you want - it all depends on your goals.

Some noteworthy goals may be the following (this is by no means a comprehensive list - add to it or create your own):

Develop a new talent/skill	Become a professional musician/performer
Enrich you life through music	Become a music teacher/educator/musicologist
Play in a band, orchestra, drumline, etc.	Compose, arrange, improvise music for movies, etc.
Create a band of your own	Write music, music books, stories, and perform them.

As a result of music lessons, you learn hand/eye coordination, dedication, determination, diligence, as well as how to focus, how to learn and how to set and achieve goals. You gain greater self confidence and purpose. You learn about perseverance and persistence, which inevitably results in a greater sense of self worth and satisfaction. There are, of course, many more rewards, but too many to list.

In setting your goals, first identify your needs and wants. Look at these questions and honestly answer them for yourself.

What do you need? Why do you need it? When do you need to obtain it? How will you obtain what you need? What do you want? Why do you want it? When do you want to obtain it? How will you obtain what you want?

Many people confuse needs and wants. They say they "need" something, when it really is a "want". They don't really need it, but they would like to have it. As you set goals for yourself, determine what you need first, and then write down as many wants as you want to. Dream a little! It's wonderful to think about the possibilities. This is not wishful thinking if it is backed up with goals (giving yourself deadlines and following through with what you plan to do). On the next page is the **Music Motivation® Mentorship Map™** followed by the **Music Motivation® Checklist™**. Use these as the starting points of your musical goals.

Become goal-oriented.
You can do anything you put your mind to.
Here's to your success!
Go! Dream Big! Make it happen! - Jerald imon (JMS)
musicmotivation.com - empoweredbypositivity.com - YouTube.com/jeraldsimon

♫ Apprentice ♫
for 1st & 2nd year students

	Music Motivation® Book(s)
Repertoire *In addition to the books listed to the right, students can sign up to receive the weekly "Cool Song" and "Cool Exercise" composed by Jerald Simon every week. Visit musicmotivation.com annual subscription to learn more and sign up!*	**Music Motivation® Book(s)** What Every Pianist Should Know (Free PDF) Essential Piano Exercises (section 1) Cool Songs for Cool Kids (pre-primer level) Cool Songs for Cool Kids (primer level) Cool Songs for Cool Kids (book 1) The Pentascale Pop Star (books 1 and 2) *Songs in Pentascale position: Classical, Jazz, Blues, Popular, Students Choice, Personal Composition (in pentascale position - 5 note piano solo) etc.*
Music Terminology	Piano (p), Forte (f) Mezzo Piano (mp) Mezzo Forte (mf) Pianissimo (pp) Fortissimo (ff) *Music Motivation® 1st Year Terminology*
Key Signatures	C, G, D, A, F, B♭, E♭ & A♭(Major) A, E, B, F♯, D, G, C & F (Minor) Begin learning all major key signatures
Music Notation	Names and Positions of notes on the staff (both hands - Treble and Bass Clefs)
Rhythms	Whole notes/rests (say it and play it - count out loud) Half notes/rests (say it and play it - count out loud) Quarter notes/rests (say it and play it - count out loud) Eighth notes/rests (say it and play it - count out loud)
Intervals	1st, 2nd, 3rd, 4th, 5th, 6th, 7th, 8th, and 9th intervals (key of C, G, D, F, B♭, and E♭). Harmonic and Melodic intervals (key of C, G, D, A, E, and B)
Scales	All Major Pentascales (5 finger scale) All Minor Pentascales (5 finger scale) All Diminished Pentascales (5 finger scale) C Major Scale (1 octave) A min. Scale (1 oct.) (Do, Re, Mi, Fa, Sol, La, Ti, Do) (solfege) All Major and Natural Minor Scales - 1 octave
Modes	Ionian/Aeolian (C/A, G/E, D/B, A/F♯)
Chords	All Major Chords, All Minor Chords, All Diminished Chords, C Sus 2, C Sus 4, C+ (Aug.), C 6th, C minor 6th, C 7th, C Maj. 7th, C minor Major 7th, A min., A Sus 2, A Sus 4,
Arpeggios	Same chords as above (1 - 2 octaves)
Inversions	Same chords as above (1 - 2 octaves)
Technique (other)	Schmitt Preparatory Exercises, (Hanon)
Sight Reading	Key of C Major and G Major
Ear Training	Major versus Minor sounds (chords/intervals)
Music History	The origins of the Piano Forte
Improvisation	Mary Had a Little Lamb, Twinkle, Twinkle...
Composition	5 note melody (both hands - key of C and G)

I try to give piano students a road map to piano success and how to improve and progress on the piano.

I created three distinct levels of progression for piano students. They are:

Level 1 - The Apprentice Stage
Level 2 - The Maestro Stage
Level 3 - The Virtuoso Stage

Within each of these stages I have created music books featuring original piano music I have composed specifically designed to teach music theory the fun way. I refer to this as the Practical Application of Music Theory.

I have created three music books that align with these three stages and countless additional supplemental books to help piano teachers and piano students enjoy playing the piano - the fun way!

The books are:

How to Play Piano the FUN Way - The Apprentice Stage
How to Play Piano the FUN Way - The Maestro Stage
How to Play Piano the FUN Way - The Virtuoso Stage

These books feature COOL SONGS and Essential Piano Exercises I have created to help piano students learn how to play piano the fun way and also learn, what I have come to learn, are the three most neglected areas in all of piano teaching.

As I do workshops with piano teachers and music educators across the country, working with countless music schools, universities, piano teaching associations, and independent piano teachers, I have found everyone - including the piano teachers, want to learn more about these three areas. They are: 1. Music Theory, 2. Improvisation, and 3. Composition. These are often the most misunderstood areas of musicianship and far too frequently the least taught areas as well.

I refer to them as:

1. Theory Therapy
2. Innovative Improvsation
3. Creative Composition

In order to help piano students and piano teachers or any music educator better understand how to learn and teach these areas of expertise, I have created additional supplemental books to augment my own piano teaching and help others.

These are some of the books from my best-selling Essential Piano Exercises Series:

Essential Piano Exercises Every Piano Player Should Know

Essential Jazz Piano Exercises Every Piano Player Should Know

Essential POP Piano Exercises Every Piano Player Should Know

Essential New Age Piano Exercises Every Piano Player Should Know

100 Left Hand Patterns Every Piano Player Should Know

An Introduction to Scales and Modes

Here are some additional fun music books I have created that feature original compositions I have composed:

Wintertide
Sweet Melancholy
Sea Fever
Triumphant
Ghosts and Goblins and Freaks and Ghouls
Sand Castles
Castles in the Sky
Adventure Awaits
Hymns of Exaltation
Peace and Serenity
Platinum
I Want to Do What Jesus Taught
Jingle those Bells
Jazzed about Christmas
Jazzed about 4th of July
Variations on Mary Had a Little Lamb

I am continually creating new music books and courses to help piano students and piano teachers. Learn more on my website at musicmotivation.com.

♪ Maestro ♪ for 2nd - 4th year students	♪ Virtuoso ♪ for 3rd year students and above
Music Motivation® Book(s)	**Music Motivation® Book(s)**
Essential Piano Exercises (section 2) An Introduction to Scales and Modes Cool Songs for Cool Kids (book 2) Cool Songs for Cool Kids (book 3) Variations on Mary Had a Little Lamb Twinkle Those Stars, Jazzed about Christmas, Jazzed about 4th of July Baroque, Romantic, Classical, Jazz, Blues, Popular, New Age, Student's Choice, Personal Composition.	Essential Piano Exercises (section 3) Cool Songs that ROCK! (books 1 & 2) Triumphant, Sea Fever, Sweet Melancholy, The Dawn of a New Age, Sweet Modality, Jazzed about Jazz, Jazzed about Classical Music, Jingle Those Bells, Cinematic Solos, Hymn Arranging Baroque, Romantic, Classical, Jazz, Blues, Popular, New Age, Contemporary, Broadway Show Tunes, Standards, Student's Choice, Personal Composition
Tempo Markings Dynamic Markings Parts of the Piano Styles and Genres of Music *Music Motivation® 2nd Year Terminology*	Pocket Music Dictionary (2 - 3 years) Harvard Dictionary of Music (4 + years) Parts/History of the Piano Music Composers (Weekly Biographies) *Music Motivation® 3rd Year Terminology*
Circle of 5ths/Circle of 4ths All Major and Minor key signatures (Identify each key and name the sharps and flats)	Spiral of Fifths, Chord Progressions within Key Signatures. Modulating from one Key Signature to another.
Names and Positions of notes above and below the staff (both hands)	History of Music Notation (the development of notation), Monks & Music, Gregorian Chants, Music changes over the years and how music has changed. Learn **Finale** and **Logic Pro** (notate your music)
Sixteenth notes/rests (say it and play it - count out loud) Thirty-second notes/rests (say it and play it - count out loud) Sixty-fourth notes/rests (say it and play it - count out loud)	One-hundred-twenty-eighth notes/rests For more on rhythm, I recommend: "Rhythmic Training" by Robert Starer and "Logical Approach to Rhythmic Notation" (books 1 & 2) by Phil Perkins
All Perfect, Major, Minor, Augmented, and Diminished intervals (in every key) All Harmonic and Melodic intervals Explain the intervals used to create major, minor, diminished, and augmented chords?	9th, 11th, and 13th intervals Analyze music (Hymns and Classical) to identify intervals used in each measure. Identify/Name intervals used in chords.
All Major Scales (Every Key 1 - 2 octaves) All Minor Scales (Every Key 1 - 2 octaves) (natural, harmonic, and melodic minor scales) (Do, Di, Re, Ri, Mi, Fa, Fi, Sol, Si, La, Li, Ti, Do) (solfege - chromatic)	All Major Scales (Every Key 3 - 5 Octaves) All Minor Scales (Every Key 3 - 5 Octaves) All Blues Scales (major and minor) Cultural Scales (25 + scales)
All Modes (I, D, P, L, M, A, L) All keys	Modulating with the Modes (Dorian to Dorian)
All Major, Minor, Diminished, Augmented, Sus 2, Sus 4, Sixth, Minor Sixth, Dominant 7th and Major 7th Chords	Review All Chords from 1st and 2nd year experiences All 7th, 9th, 11th, and 13th chords inversions and voicings.
Same chords as above (3 - 4 octaves)	Same chords as above (4 + octaves)
Same chords as above (3 - 4 octaves)	Same chords as above (4 + octaves)
Wieck, Hanon, Bach (well tempered clavier)	Bertini-Germer, Czerny, I. Philipp
Key of C, G, D, A, E, F, B♭, E♭, A♭, D♭	All Key Signatures, Hymns, Classical
C, D, E, F, G, A, B, and intervals	Key Signatures and Chords, Play w/ IPod
Baroque, Classical, Jazz, Blues	Students choice - All genres, Composers
Blues Pentascale, Barrelhouse Blues	Classical, New Age, Jazz, Blues, etc. Play w/ IPod
One - Two Page Song (include key change)	Lyrical, Classical, New Age, Jazz, etc.

Learn how to play the following on the piano (in every key signature)...

Below is a list of what I suggest all piano players should be able to do in all key signatures and in all inversions. These are all written out in every key signature in my book, **"Essential Piano Exercises Every Piano Player Should Know"**:

- **All Intervals** (Harmonic and Melodic)
- **All Major Pentascales** in every key signature
- **All Minor Pentascales** in every key signature
- **All Diminished Pentascales** in every key signature
- **All Tetra Chords** for all keys
- **All Major and Minor Scales** (natural, harmonic, and melodic) 1, 2, and 3 octaves in every key signature
- **All Major and Minor Scales** contrary and parallel motion - 1, 2, and 3 octaves in every key signature
- **All Major Triads** (root, first, and second inversions) in every key signature
- **All Minor Triads** (root, first, and second inversions) in every key signature
- **All Diminished Triads** (root, first, and second inversions) in every key signature
- **All Augmented Triads** (root, first, and second inversions) in every key signature
- **All Sus4 Triads** (root, first, and second inversions) in every key signature
- **All Sus2 Triads** (root, first, and second inversions) in every key signature
- **All 6th Chords** (root, first, second, and third inversions) in every key signature
- **All Minor 6th Chords** (root, first, second, and third inversions) in every key signature
- **All Major 7th Chords** (root, first, second, and third inversions) in every key signature
- **All Minor Major 7th Chords** (root, first, second, and third inversions) in every key signature
- **All 7th Chords** (root, first, second, and third inversions) in every key signature
- **All Minor 7th Chords** (root, first, second, and third inversions) in every key signature
- **All Minor 7 Flat 5 Chords** (root, first, second, and third inversions) in every key signature
- **All Minor 7 Sharp 5 Chords** (root, first, second, and third inversions) in every key signature
- **All Diminished 7th Chords** (root, first, second, and third inversions) in every key signature
- **I - IV - V - V7 - I Chord Progression** (in every inversion and in every key signature)
- **i - iv - V - V7 - i Chord Progression** (in every inversion and in every key signature)
- **All Triads Built from the Major Scales** (in every inversion and in every key signature)
- **All 7th Chords** (moving up diatonically) in every key signature
- **All Major Octave** Chords in every key signature

In addition to the above, you should also be able to play the following:

- **All Major Blues Scales** in every key signature
- **All Minor Blues Scales** in every key signature
- **All Major Pentatonic Scales** in every key signature
- **All Modes** (i.e. Ionian, Dorian, Phrygian, Lydian, Mixolydian, Aeolian, Locrian) in every key signature
- **All 9th Chords, 11th Chords, and 13th Chords** in every voicing and in every key signature

This is just a simple outline to get you going. There is actually so much more we can learn that we could include in our list, but the list would turn into an entire book or many more books (which they may). In this book I have taught basic and fundamental jazz piano exercises in a fun way through original jazz pieces I have composed. Both the jazz pieces and jazz exercises are essentially just jazz patterns and I hope you have had fun playing these essential jazz piano exercises!

A Few Additional Ideas for Piano Teachers and Parents of Piano Students

You can visit this link to read the original blog post from which this excerpt below was created: (https://www.musicmotivation.com/blog/don-t-teach-music-theory-unless-you-teach-the-practical-application).

In the blog post, I talked specifically about 10 steps to begin teaching the practical application of music theory so students know their theory inside and out. I thought I would share the 10 steps here from the blog post:

Before any piano student plays their piece, I believe they should be able to do the following (this is what I try to have my students do with their music):

1. Tell their music teacher the key signature and time signature.

2. Identify all of the sharps or flats in the key signature.

3. Play all of the intervals created from the major key signature of the piece they are playing - this is more for piano students and possibly guitar students, as many instruments only allow one note at a time. If the student is younger or new to their instrument, they can play the intervals created from the pentascales or five note scales created from the first five notes of the major or minor scales.

4. Play through the major scale of the key signature of the piece at least 1-2 octaves up and down the piano (parallel and or contrary motion). If the student is younger or new to their instrument, as stated before, they can play the pentascales, or five note scales created from the first five notes of the major or minor scales.

5. Play what I refer to as the "Essential Piano Exercises" from each key signature. (In the blog post I show an example from the key of C major from my book "Essential Piano Exercises" - Intervals, Scales, and Chords in all Keys and in all Inversions - a 288 page book with all intervals, scales, and simple triads and 6th and 7th chords in all keys and inversions).

These are the other 5 steps:

Once a student can do the above five essential "getting started steps" in any given key signature (and many times I will do the following steps even if they can't do the above steps in every key signature), I then challenge them to do the following five essential "music theory application steps."

1. Once the student has learned and perfected the piece, ask him or her to take the song up half a step and down half a step. In the beginning, this is a good start. Later on, when they are better able to do so, have the student play the piece in any key signature. Start with simple pieces like "Mary Had a Little Lamb" and "Twinkle, Twinkle, Little Star." Have the students try playing these in all key signatures.

2. Ask the student to come up with at least 5-10 variations or arrangements of their piece.

3. Ask the student to compose 3 or 4 motifs (or single melodic line or phrase), and then put them together. This can be the beginning of creating a simple piece. I have students begin using scales and skipping notes here and there. We then have them take a simple pattern created from the notes of the major scale (1 2 3 4 5 6 7 8).

4. Ask the student to "Play a Rainbow." When I say this to students, I then begin to ask them to "play" anything. I may say: "Play me a shadow," "Play me a swing set," "Play me a thunderstorm," or "Play me a puddle, a rock, a tree, a meadow, a light, etc.". The sky is the limit. I first begin with tangible objects and eventually move on to intangible ideas and concepts, such as "Play me loneliness," "Play me disturbed, agitated, angered, humbled, pensive, etc.". Again, the sky is the limit. It is wonderful to see what students can create, even if they don't know all the rules of composition or terminology. Everyone has music within them.

5. I have students begin notating their music. I enjoy and prefer Finale, but that is because I have used it for so long and am familiar with it. There are many great programs available. After we have their music put down on paper, I then export the music from Finale as a midi file and open the midi file in Logic Pro. We then begin having them add additional instruments so they can create background tracks (this is how I create all of my weekly "**Cool Songs**" from my **COOL SONGS Series** (you can learn more about my COOL SONGS Series at this link: https://musicmotivation.com/coolsongs/). The students then have a PDF copy of their composition and an MP3 "minus track" to accompany them as they play. Talk about music motivation!

These are the books included in the COOL SONGS Series: https://musicmotivation.com/coolsongs/ -

The Apprentice Stage - The Maestro Stage - The Virtuoso Stage

COOL SONGS for COOL KIDS (Primer Level) by Jerald Simon
COOL SONGS for COOL KIDS (book 1) by Jerald Simon
COOL SONGS for COOL KIDS (book 2) by Jerald Simon
COOL SONGS for COOL KIDS (book 3) by Jerald Simon
COOL SONGS that ROCK! (book 1) by Jerald Simon
COOL SONGS that ROCK! (book 2) by Jerald Simon

Join the Essential Piano Exercises Course by Jerald Simon
https://www.essentialpianoexercises.com

Gain lifetime access to the PDF books listed on the website above (which also includes video piano lesson tutorials where Jerald Simon demonstrates examples from the books and gives piano pointers, tips to try, and the practical application of music theory). I demonstrate how to use the music theory to arrange and compose music of your own!

This course features pre-recorded video lessons so you can watch and learn how to play the piano at your convenience. You choose when and where you learn to play the piano.

Join the **Essential Piano Exercises Course** and receive the following PDF books along with access to the monthly video lesson taught by Jerald Simon for a one time payment of $199.95.

Join the **Essential Piano Exercises Course** by Jerald Simon

EssentialPianoExercises.com

Gain lifetime access to the following PDF books (which include video piano lesson tutorials where Jerald Simon demonstrates examples from the book and gives piano pointers, tips to try, and the practical application of music theory where Jerald demonstrates how to use the music theory!

This course features pre-recorded video lessons so you can watch and learn how to play the piano at your convenience. You choose when and where you learn to play the piano.

This Course features the following books (included as PDF downloads with the course):

1. **Essential Piano Exercises Every Piano Player Should Know - PDF book and Video Course**
2. **100 Left Hand Patterns Every Piano Player Should Know - PDF book and Video Course**
3. **Essential Jazz Piano Exercises Every Piano Player Should Know - PDF book and Video Course**
4. **Essential New Age Piano Exercises Every Piano Player Should Know - PDF book and Video Course**
5. **Essential POP Piano Exercises Every Piano Player Should Know - PDF book and Video Course**
6. **Essential FAKE BOOK Fundamentals Every Piano Player Should Know - PDF book and Course**
7. **100 Chord Progressions Every Piano Player Should Know - PDF book and Video Course**
8. **Jazzed about Jazz - PDF book and Video Course**
9. **Jazzed about Christmas - PDF book and Video Course**
10. **Jazzed about 4th of July - PDF book and Video Course**
11. **Innovative Improvisation Ideas Every Piano Player Should Know - PDF book and Video Course**

In addition to having access to these PDF books and Video Courses, the following will be added to your lifetime account:

- Anyone who has purchased the Essential Piano Exercises course will continue to have access to all of the PDF books, video lesson tutorials, power point presentations, and handouts. New books from the Essential Piano Exercises Series, additional MP3s, new video lessons, and monthly training seminars, webinars, and additional resources will be added for the current members of the Essential Piano Exercises monthly subscription group.
- Access to the Essential Piano Exercises Facebook group - a private Facebook group created only for the members of the Essential Piano Exercises course. By joining the Facebook group you will have access to additional live piano lessons every month taught by Jerald Simon. Monthly piano pointers, tips to try, and short video lessons will be shared throughout the month for the members of the Facebook group.

youtube.com/jeraldsimon

I upload new videos on Wednesdays, and Fridays on my YouTube channel, **youtube.com/jeraldsimon**. I have a few different playlists filled with great content for beginning - advanced piano students. The videos are geared for everyone from brand new piano students to music majors, professional pianists, and piano teachers of all skill levels.

There are three main playlists for my **free on-line piano lessons.** I do offer in person piano lessons, Zoom/FaceTime piano lessons, and step by step piano lesson packages you can purchase and watch at home (https://www.musicmotivation.com/pianolessons), but the ones listed below are FREE to everyone who subscribes to my YouTube channel:

1. **PIANO FUNdamentals** (emphasis on the word FUN!)
2. **5 Minute Piano Lessons with Jerald Simon** (sponsored by Music Motivation®)
3. **Theory Tip Tuesday Piano Lessons**

I frequently release new videos. Some are piano lessons, and others are filmed recordings of workshops, masterclasses, or concerts. I also have these additional types of videos on my YouTube channel:

a. **Meditation/Relaxation Music Composed by Jerald Simon**
b. **Hymn Arrangements by Jerald Simon**
c. **Motivational Messages by Jerald Simon**
d. **Motivational Poetry by Jerald Simon**
e. **Theory Tip Tuesday (FREE Weekly Piano Lesson Videos) by Jerald Simon**
f. **Cool Songs by Jerald Simon (musicmotivation.com/coolsongs)**
g. **Assemblies, Workshops, Firesides, and more...**

Let me know if you have a tutorial you'd like me to come out with to better help you learn the piano. I'm happy to help in any way I can and love hearing feedback from others about what they personally are looking for in piano lesson videos to help them learn to play the piano better. I primarily focus on music theory, improvisation/arranging, and composition. I refer to these as **THEORY THERAPY, INNOVATIVE IMPROVISATION, and CREATIVE COMPOSITION**.

I have also produced hundreds of COOL SONGS that teach students music theory the fun way. If you'd like to learn more about the COOL SONGS, that I composed to motivate my own piano students, or if you would like to purchase the COOL SONGS series featuring the music/books, simply visit musicmotivation.com/coolsongs to be taken to the page on my website that explains a little more about the COOL SONGS. You can also watch piano video tutorial lessons featuring 85 of the 200 + COOL SONGS (youtube.com/jeraldsimon). Let me know what you think. I'd love your feedback about the music. It helps me as I compose more COOL SONGS to motivate more piano students. I'm excited to have you watch my free video piano lessons on YouTube.com/jeraldsimon.

Perceptions, Parables, and Pointers by JERALD SIMON (read more at this link): http://musicmotivation.com/shop/motivationalself-help-books/perceptions-parables-and-pointers-by-jerald-simon/

What do you really want to do with your time? What is your mission in life? Where have you been, and where would you like to go? What are your dreams, your hopes, and your wishes? If you could do anything in the world, what would it be?

The main goal in writing down these perceptions, parables, and pointers, and in creating this book in general, is to present ideas that will help get people thinking, imagining, planning, creating, and actively participating in life.

The "As If" Principle (motivational poetry) by JERALD SIMON features 222 original motivational poems written by Simon to inspire and motivate men, women, businesses, organizations, leaders, mentors, advisers, teachers, and students. The poems were written to teach values and encourage everyone everywhere to do and be their best. (read more at this link): http://musicmotivation.com/shop/motivationalself-help-books/the-as-if-principle-by-jerald-simon/

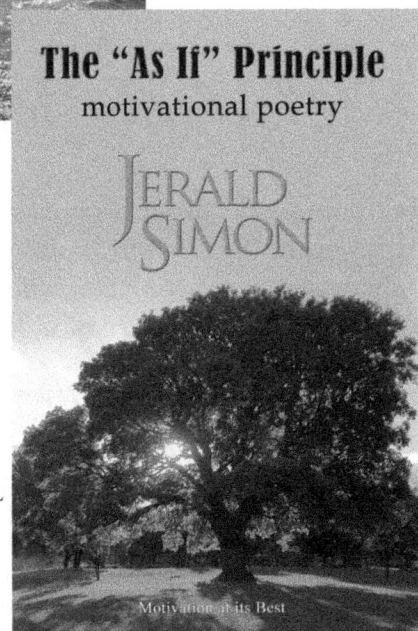

Jerald's Albums & Singles
are available from all online music stores

Stream Jerald's music on
Pandora, Spotify, iTunes, Amazon, and all streaming sites.

and many more...

Check out Jerald's Cool Song Piano Package

Jerald continually produces and releases new "Cool Songs" available for all piano students and piano teachers on his website (*musicmotivation.com*). Each new *"Cool Song"* is emailed to Music Motivation® mentees (piano teachers and piano students) who have are signed up for his weekly online piano lessons he teaches. See which subscription is the best fit for you and for your piano students (if you are a piano teacher) by visiting:

https://www.musicmotivation.com/pianolessons

At **Music Motivation**®, I strive to produce the best quality products I can to help musicians of all ages better understand music theory (Theory Therapy), improvisation (Innovative Improvisation), and composition (Creative Composition). I try to tailor my products around the needs of piano teachers and piano students of all ages - from beginning through advanced and would love to receive your feedback about what I can do to better help you teach and learn. Let me know if there is a type of piano music, music book, fun audio or video tutorial, or any other educational product you would like to see in the field of music (principally the piano), but have not yet found, that would help you teach and learn the piano better. Please contact me. I look forward to your comments and suggestions. Thank you.

Check out these best sellers by Jerald Simon

Learn more about
JERALD SIMON

Visit https://www.musicmotivation.com/jeraldsimon

"My purpose and mission in life is to motivate myself and others through my music and writing, to help others find their purpose and mission in life, and to teach values and encourage everyone everywhere to do and be their best." - Jerald Simon

First and foremost, Jerald is a husband to his beautiful wife, Zanny, and a father to his wonderful children. Jerald Simon is the founder of **Music Motivation®** (musicmotivation.com), a company he formed to provide music instruction through workshops, giving speeches and seminars, concerts and performances in the field of music and motivation. He is a composer, author, poet, and Music Mentor/piano teacher (primarily focusing his piano teaching on music theory, improvisation, composition, and arranging). Jerald loves spending time with his wife, Zanny, and their children. In addition, he loves music, teaching, speaking, performing, playing sports, exercising, reading, writing poetry and self help books, and gardening.

Jerald Simon is the founder of **Music Motivation®** and focuses on helping piano students and piano teachers learn music theory, improvisation, and composition. He refers to these areas as: **Theory Therapy™, Innovative Improvisation™, and Creative Composition™.** Simon is an author and composer and has written 30 music books featuring almost 300 original compositions, 15 albums (you can listen to Jerald's music on Pandora, Spotify, iTunes, Amazon, and all online music stations. Jerald's books and CDs are also available from Amazon, Wal-Mart.com, Barnes and Noble and all major retail outlets). He has published three motivational poetry books featuring over 400 original poems (poetrythatmotivates.com), and is the creator of the best-selling **Cool Songs Series** (musicmotivation.com/coolsongs), the best-selling **Essential Piano Exercises Series** (essentialpianoexercises.com) and Essential Piano Lessons for piano students (essentialpianolessons.com). He has also created **Essential Piano Teachers** for piano teachers (essentialpianoteachers.com). You can watch Jerald's videos on his YouTube channel at: youtube.com/jeraldsimon. Listen to Jerald's music on all streaming sites and his podcast, **Music, Motivation, and More – The Positivity Podcast** with Jerald Simon on all podcast platforms.

In 2008, Jerald began creating his Cool Songs to help teach music theory – the FUN way, by putting FUN back into theory FUNdamentals. Jerald has also filmed hundreds of piano lesson video tutorials on his YouTube page (youtube.com/jeraldsimon). In addition to music books and albums, he is the author/poet of **"The As If Principle"** (motivational poetry), and the books **"Perceptions, Parables, and Pointers," "Motivation in a Minute,"** and **"Who Are You?"**.

SPECIALTIES:

Composer, Author, Poet, Music Mentor, Piano Teacher (jazz, music theory, improvisation, composition, arranging, etc.), Motivational Speaker, and Life Coach. Visit https://www.musicmotivation.com/, to book Jerald as a speaker/performer. Visit https://www.musicmotivation.com/ to print off FREE piano resources for piano teachers and piano students.

Book me to speak/perform for your group or for a concert or performance:

jeraldsimon@musicmotivation.com - (801)644-0540 - https://www.musicmotivation.com/

www.ingramcontent.com/pod-product-compliance
Lightning Source LLC
LaVergne TN
LVHW061341060426
835511LV00014B/2044